FLORIDA

FLORIDA

HELLO
U.S.A.

by Karen Sirvaitis

Lerner Publications Company

You'll find this picture of oranges at the beginning of each chapter. With its warm climate and abundant sunshine, Florida is able to produce oranges and other citrus fruits. In fact, the state of Florida produces about two-thirds of the nation's oranges, which are sold across the country as fruit and in products such as juice and jelly.

Cover (left): Clearwater Beach. Cover (right): An alligator lies in the grass in the Everglades. Pages 2–3: Overview of Miami Beach and Biscayne Bay. Page 3: Two scarlet macaws perched on a branch at Walt Disney World in Orlando.

This book is available in two editions:
Library binding by Lerner Publications Company, a division of Lerner Publishing Group
Soft cover by First Avenue Editions, an imprint of Lerner Publishing Group
241 First Avenue North
Minneapolis, MN 55401 U.S.A.

Website address: www.lernerbooks.com

Library of Congress Cataloging-in-Publication Data

Sirvaitis, Karen, 1961–
    Florida / by Karen Sirvaitis (Rev. and expanded 2nd ed.)
        p.   cm. — (Hello U.S.A.)
    Includes index.
    Summary: Introduces the geography, history, environment, economy, and culture of the Sunshine State.
    ISBN: 0–8225–4066–5 (lib. bdg. : alk paper)
    ISBN: 0–8225–4144–0 (pbk. : alk. paper)
    1. Florida—Juvenile literature. [1. Florida.] I. Title. II. Series.
    F311.3 .S49 2002
    975.9—dc21   2001002959

Manufactured in the United States of America
1 2 3 4 5 6 – JR – 07 06 05 04 03 02

CONTENTS

Windsurfing is a popular sport in Florida.

THE LAND

Peninsula and Panhandle

Because Florida is a peninsula, there are many long beaches for vacationers to enjoy.

Beach balls, oranges, and sunny days. These images of Florida match the state's nickname—the Sunshine State. Florida's many days of sunshine are such an attraction that some stores in the state sell cans that supposedly are filled with the warm, bright light.

Florida is a southern state. Georgia and Alabama are Florida's neighbors to the north, but most of Florida has borders that change with the tide. The powerful waves of the Atlantic Ocean wash against the state's eastern shore, while the Gulf of Mexico laps against the western shore. At the southern end of the state flows the Straits of Florida, a waterway that connects the Gulf and the ocean.

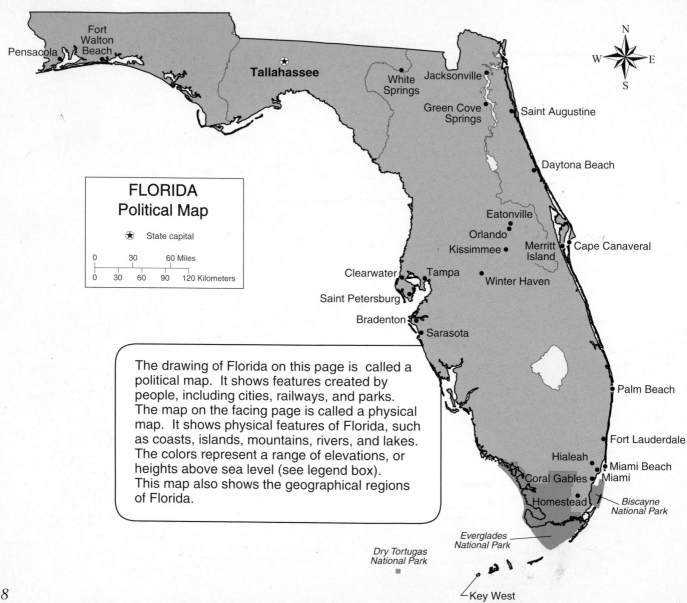

FLORIDA
Political Map

✪ State capital

| 0 | | 30 | | 60 Miles |
| 0 | 30 | 60 | 90 | 120 Kilometers |

The drawing of Florida on this page is called a political map. It shows features created by people, including cities, railways, and parks. The map on the facing page is called a physical map. It shows physical features of Florida, such as coasts, islands, mountains, rivers, and lakes. The colors represent a range of elevations, or heights above sea level (see legend box). This map also shows the geographical regions of Florida.

Pensacola
Fort Walton Beach
Tallahassee
White Springs
Jacksonville
Green Cove Springs
Saint Augustine
Daytona Beach
Eatonville
Orlando
Kissimmee
Merritt Island
Cape Canaveral
Clearwater
Tampa
Winter Haven
Saint Petersburg
Bradenton
Sarasota
Palm Beach
Fort Lauderdale
Hialeah
Miami Beach
Coral Gables
Miami
Homestead
Biscayne National Park
Everglades National Park
Dry Tortugas National Park
Key West

N
W E
S

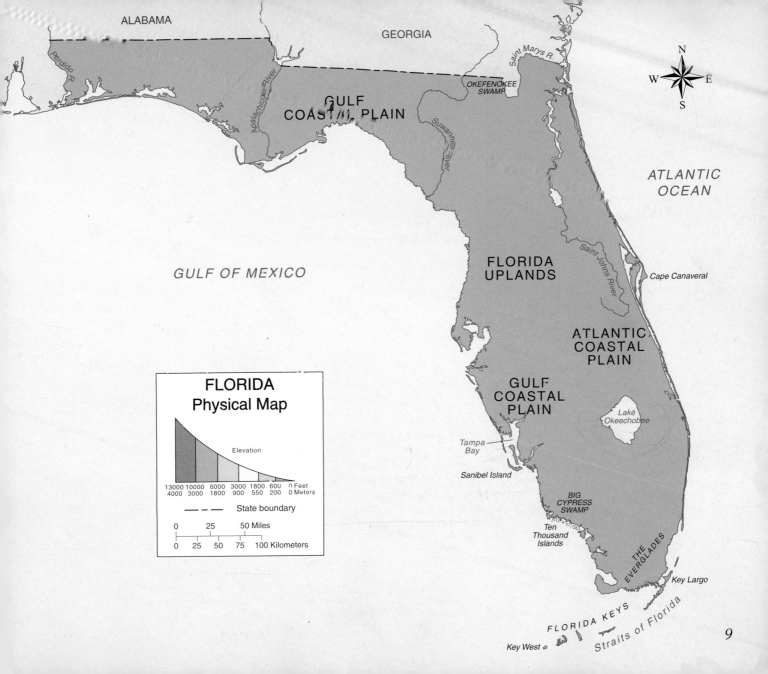

ALABAMA

GEORGIA

Perdido R.

Apalachicola River

GULF COASTAL PLAIN

Saint Marys R.

OKEFENOKEE SWAMP

Suwannee River

N
W E
S

FLORIDA UPLANDS

Saint Johns River

ATLANTIC OCEAN

Cape Canaveral

GULF OF MEXICO

ATLANTIC COASTAL PLAIN

GULF COASTAL PLAIN

Lake Okeechobee

Tampa Bay

Sanibel Island

BIG CYPRESS SWAMP

Ten Thousand Islands

THE EVERGLADES

Key Largo

FLORIDA KEYS

Straits of Florida

Key West

FLORIDA
Physical Map

Elevation

| 13000 | 10000 | 6000 | 3000 | 1800 | 600 | 0 Feet |
| 4000 | 3000 | 1800 | 900 | 550 | 200 | 0 Meters |

– – –   State boundary

0   25   50 Miles
0   25   50   75   100 Kilometers

9

A number of Florida's small islands are made up of coral A damselfish *(left)* swims over sponges that have grown on a coral reef.

Most of Florida is surrounded by water on three sides, forming a **peninsula.** The northernmost section of the state is called a panhandle because it is shaped somewhat like the handle of a frying pan. Florida's outline makes it one of the most noticeable states on the map, but Florida has not always been so easy to find. At one time, in fact, its land lay entirely under water.

Millions of years ago, Florida was an island. Volcanoes spewed out bubbling hot lava, threatening the island's plant life. The island was eventually buried by rising seawater, only to reappear as the level of the sea lowered. **Coral reefs**—colorful underwater layers of limestone—began to form along the coast.

The grassy plains of the Florida Uplands make the region a perfect place for horse ranches.

For thousands of years, the sea level rose and fell, covering and then exposing Florida's coastline. The movement of the seawater helped form three land regions in the state—the Atlantic Coastal Plain, the Florida Uplands, and the Gulf Coastal Plain.

The Atlantic Coastal Plain, much of which is low and flat, stretches from north to south along eastern Florida. The region includes an offshore strip of sandbars (ridges of sand) and islands that protect the coast from being thrashed by ocean waves. Shallow bodies of water called lagoons and grassy wetlands called **marshes** are sandwiched between the islands and the sparkling white coastal sands of the mainland.

The Florida Keys are situated at the southern tip of the Atlantic Coastal Plain. These islands curve through the Straits of Florida into the Gulf of Mexico.

The Florida Uplands region runs across the northern half of the Panhandle and then cuts down into north central Florida, dividing the Gulf Coastal Plain into two parts. The northern uplands are hilly, and the southern portion of the region contains many shallow lakes.

Everglades National Park includes the Ten Thousand Islands, a group of small islands in the Gulf of Mexico.

A young Floridian plays on the Gulf of Mexico during the summer.

The Gulf Coastal Plain covers almost all of western Florida. One section of this marshy region arcs across the southern portion of the Panhandle. The other half covers the southwestern part of the peninsula. Over the years, many of the area's marshes have been drained and filled with sand and soil to make the land solid enough to support homes and other structures.

But Florida is still home to some of the most famous wetlands in the nation. Big Cypress Swamp and the Everglades cover much of southern Florida. The Okefenokee Swamp straddles the border between Georgia and Florida.

Swamps are not the only inland bodies of water in Florida. The state's largest lake is Okeechobee, which covers nearly 700 square miles of southern Florida. Like most of Florida's lakes, Lake Okeechobee is quite shallow. Its average depth is only about 8 feet. Florida's largest river is the Saint Johns. Other chief rivers include the Apalachicola, the Perdido, and the Saint Marys.

Breezes from the Atlantic Ocean and from the Gulf of Mexico cool Florida during the long, hot, and humid summers. But even so, summer temperatures throughout the state average a steamy 83° F. During the winter, Floridians experience some relief from the heat. Winter temperatures average 67° F throughout the peninsula. Along the Panhandle, temperatures are slightly cooler.

Every summer and fall, tropical storms that produce severe winds, heavy rainfall, and high waves threaten Florida. Called hurricanes, these storms cause ocean waves to swell and flood coastal areas, sometimes bringing about many deaths and billions of dollars in damages.

A rainbow appears as
rain clouds move away.

Rainstorms are common in Florida. About 54
inches of rain fall each year in the state, some of it
in the form of pounding thunderstorms. But the
storm clouds quickly clear, permitting the Sunshine
State to live up to its nickname.

Misty mornings add to Florida's natural beauty.

Florida's generally warm and clear weather suits
a variety of plants and animals. Mangroves—short
trees whose jumbled-up roots crave salty ocean
water—grow well along the coasts. Palm trees and
forests of beech, bald cypress, magnolia, and pine
cover about half the state. Beautiful tropical
flowers, including orchids and lilies, grow wild
in Florida.

Florida is home to large populations of waterbirds, including pelicans, herons, and flamingos. Black bears, deer, foxes, and wildcats roam Florida's forests. Bass, catfish, bluefish, marlins, red snappers, and sharks are common to the state's waters. Shellfish such as clams, crabs, crayfish, and oysters are found along the coasts. The endangered Florida manatee lives in shallow coastal waters. Alligators prowl through Florida's lakes, swamps, and rivers.

Brown pelicans are one of Florida's many types of waterfowl.

THE HISTORY

Natives and Newcomers

he story of the first Floridians is a mystery. No one is certain when they arrived or where they came from. But many researchers believe that American Indians, or Native Americans, first reached the peninsula about 12,000 years ago. Some of them walked from the north. Others may have crossed the seas from the south.

Eventually, at least four major Native American nations, or tribes, made their homes in the area's forests and swamplands. The Calusa and the Tequesta lived in the south, and the Timucua and the Apalachee settled in the north. All four Indian groups used poles as frames for their homes. The branches of palmettos (palm trees with fan-shaped leaves) served as roofs.

Disguised in a deer hide, a Timucua hunter prepares to attack his prey.

The Indians of Florida were skilled hunters and fishers. Using blowguns, bows and arrows, and clubs, hunters killed bears, wild turkeys, deer, and alligators to feed and clothe village members. Fishers speared their catch or trapped many fish at a time with fences placed underwater.

The Timucua and the Apalachee were good farmers as well, harvesting squash, corn, beans, and pumpkins. The Calusa and the Tequesta paddled dugout canoes southward to the Caribbean islands, where they traded goods with other tribes.

Maize, or corn, was a popular crop for early Florida farmers because it could be stored all winter long without spoiling.

At least 100,000 American Indians lived in Florida in 1513, when Spanish explorers landed off the Atlantic coast near what later became Saint Augustine. Legend has it that the adventurers, led by Juan Ponce de León, were seeking the Fountain of Youth. The waters of this magical spring were rumored to restore health and youth to the sick and elderly.

The Timucua cooked the game they hunted by smoking it over an open fire.

A Florida legend says that Ponce de León *(lower right)* came to Florida in search of the Fountain of Youth.

Whether the Spaniards actually searched for the fountain is not known for certain. Historians do know, however, that the Spaniards were looking for gold. When Ponce de León did not find any gold, he left Florida. He returned in 1521, only to be wounded in a battle with the Calusa. The magical waters that Ponce de León needed to cure himself were nowhere to be found, and the explorer died shortly afterward.

During the following 40 years, other Spanish explorers looking for gold and other treasures came to Florida. They tried several times to set up a Spanish **colony,** or settlement, there. All the colonies failed, conquered mainly by the wilderness, brutal weather, and fatal illness.

Unknown in Europe, the alligator was one of many new dangers that Spanish explorers found in Florida.

23

Huguenots arrived
in Florida in 1564.

In 1564 Huguenots—a group of people who had
left France to find religious freedom—built Fort
Caroline, near what later became Jacksonville.
From this northeastern site, the French were in a
good position to attack and loot Spanish ships.
These ships were sailing from South America loaded
with gold and silver.

One year later, Spain sent Captain Pedro
Menéndez de Avilés to drive the French out of
Florida. Menéndez and his soldiers massacred most

of the French settlers, who were caught unprotected at Fort Caroline. He then founded a Spanish settlement called Saint Augustine. The settlement firmly established Florida as a Spanish colony.

The Spaniards were very religious. They preached to the Indians, trying to persuade them to give up their own religious beliefs and to become Catholics. Some Indians became Catholic, but most did not. Many were punished for refusing to convert.

From the mid-1500s to the mid-1700s, the Spaniards fought off many attackers, including the French and the British. Britain, which had established its own colonies along the Atlantic coast to the north of Florida, was one of Spain's oldest enemies and was eager for more land. During these attacks, hundreds of Indians living in Florida were captured and taken north to be sold as slaves in the British colonies.

Spanish settlers established Saint Augustine in 1565. The city was the first permanent European settlement in what later became the United States.

In 1763 Spain gave Florida to Britain in exchange for Cuba, an island south of Florida. By this time, few Indians were living in the Florida colony. Most had either died from European diseases, had been sold into slavery, or had followed the Spaniards to Cuba.

At about the same time, thousands of Creek Indians, who had been forced from their homes in Georgia and Alabama by European settlers, moved southward into Florida. The Creek in Florida became known as the Seminoles.

The British divided Florida into two colonies. East Florida had its capital at Saint Augustine, and West Florida's capital became Pensacola. Most of the British settlers who came to the two colonies planted figs, sugarcane, cotton, indigo (a plant that yields a blue dye), and rice—crops suited to Florida's climate. Many of the people who labored on the colonies' **plantations,** or large farms, were black slaves from Africa.

In 1775 colonists in 13 of Britain's North American colonies began fighting the American Revolution against Great Britain. The colonies no

Many Floridians claim to be descendants of people who were brought from Greece and Minorca (a Spanish island) to work on rice farms. Rice was first grown in Florida in the mid-1700s.

longer wanted to be ruled by a faraway king. They wanted instead to govern themselves.

The Floridas, however, stayed almost completely out of the revolution. Most Floridians had just recently left Britain for Florida, so they still felt loyal to the British king. In addition, the Floridas depended heavily on Britain for money.

But Britain's control over the Florida colonies was short lived. While British forces were busy fighting the war, Spain captured West Florida. In 1783 Britain lost the revolution and decided to return East Florida to Spain. Meanwhile, the 13 colonies united and formed one country—the United States of America. Florida would soon fly the same flag.

When Florida became a territory of the United States in 1822, the Spanish flag was replaced with the U.S. flag.

Spanish settlers again moved into the Floridas, and so did Americans. Some Americans took over abandoned British plantations. Others built homes on Seminole land. By the early 1800s, Americans outnumbered Spaniards in the Floridas.

Angry that so many Americans were taking Indian land, the Seminoles attacked the settlers. In 1817 General Andrew Jackson led U.S. soldiers into battle against the Seminole Indians. The First Seminole War ended in 1818 with a victory for Jackson. More wars would follow.

The U.S. military intervention left Spain feeling powerless in the Floridas. In 1821 Spain decided to give the colonies to the United States for $5 million. The next year, the United States merged East and West Florida into one territory. Tallahassee was chosen as the capital city.

Once again, Americans poured into Florida. Many were farmers interested in the fertile lands of northern Florida— Seminole territory. In 1835 fights over who owned this land helped start the Second Seminole War-- the most expensive Indian conflict in U.S. history.

General Andrew Jackson briefly served as governor of the new territory.

The Seminoles fought for their land in the Second Seminole War under the leadership of Osceola (1804?–1838). Osceola led many successful attacks on U.S. troops. He died shortly after being captured in 1837.

Costing the United States at least $20 million and 1,500 lives, the conflict lasted seven years. The Seminoles also paid a heavy price. Some Seminoles fled to the Everglades, but most either died from disease or wounds or were moved far away to Oklahoma.

With most of the Indians gone, even more Americans came to Florida to grow cotton on the Panhandle and sugarcane on the peninsula. The planters brought thousands of slaves to Florida. Of the more than 45,000 people in the territory in the 1840s, half were black slaves.

Seminole Indians attack a government blockhouse.

The Seminole Freedmen

The First and Second Seminole Wars were fought over more than just land. They were also fought over the freedom of escaped slaves who came to be known as the Seminole Freedmen, or the Seminole blacks.

During and after the American Revolution, black slaves from Georgia and the Carolinas fled to Spanish Florida, where the Seminole Indians welcomed the runaways. Many of these blacks were experiencing freedom for the first time.

Because they spoke English better than most Seminoles, some Freedmen became tribal leaders and influenced decisions made by the Seminole nation.

In the early 1800s, plantation owners complained to the U.S. government that the Seminoles harbored escaped slaves. The U.S. Army tried to capture and return the runaways. The Seminoles chose to fight for the Freedmen, who were an important part of the Seminole nation. This decision sparked both Seminole wars.

Southern slaves worked long and hard at tasks such as picking cotton on plantations.

In 1845 Florida had enough white residents to become a state. On March 3, 1845, Florida became the 27th state of the Union. But by this time, the Northern and Southern states disagreed over many issues, including slavery.

Northerners, many of whom worked in factories, had outlawed slavery in their states. Southerners, however, still made a living largely from the growing and selling of crops. To be properly maintained, plantations required a large workforce. Southern planters argued that without slave labor, they could not afford to run the farms and still make a profit.

In 1861 Florida and other Southern states formed the Confederate States of America (the Confederacy), a nation where slavery would be legal. Shortly afterward, Southern forces attacked a Union fort in the Confederate state of South Carolina, and the Civil War began.

Union troops immediately captured Florida's coastal cities, but few battles were fought in the state. Florida's major role in the Civil War was to supply beef, pork, salt, and sugar to Confederate troops.

The Confederacy lost the war in 1865. Austin, in Texas, and Tallahassee were the only two Confederate state capitals that had not been occupied by Union troops. After the war, the Union made its presence known in Tallahassee and elsewhere in the South.

A period of reform called **Reconstruction** brought Northern troops, politicians, and teachers into the South to make changes. The 70,000 slaves in Florida had been freed. Schools were built for African American children, and African American men were given the right to vote and to hold public office.

Three African American state representatives were photographed on the steps of Florida's capitol in 1875. The state's House of Representatives included eight African Americans at the time.

In the late 1800s, two-fifths of Florida was soggy wetland, unsuitable for growing crops and building homes. So the state both sold its land at low prices and gave it away to anyone willing to drain the swamps and marshes and build something that would encourage people to move to the state.

Florida's government gave most of the free land to railroad companies. By train, people and goods could easily reach remote areas. And farmers could ship their citrus fruits to northern markets, where the climate was too cold for growing grapefruits and oranges.

The trains also brought tourists. Florida's warm winter weather and beautiful coastline made the state an attractive resort area for vacationers. Dozens of hotels sprang up, creating the resort towns of Miami Beach, Coral Gables, Key West, Palm Beach, Tampa, Clearwater, and Saint Petersburg. Land sales in Florida skyrocketed as people realized they could make millions of dollars selling beachfront property.

Oranges are put into crates at a Florida citrus plant in the 1800s.

Tourists flocked to Florida in the late 1800s. Elegant hotels, such as this one in Green Cove Springs, were built to serve the visitors.

By the 1890s, Florida was booming. Miners had discovered that central Florida covered large deposits of phosphate rock, a mineral used to make fertilizers. A tobacco processor named Vicente Martinez Ybor established a thriving cigar industry in Tampa. Cattle, which had originally been brought to Florida by Juan Ponce de León, were being raised on a large scale in central Florida.

In 1898 the United States became involved in a revolution taking place in Cuba, which was still ruled by Spain. Most Cubans wanted to be free of Spanish rule, and the U.S. government sided with the Cubans. During the Spanish-American War, military bases were built on Florida's coast. The state expanded its military role during World War I (1914–1918), when it became a major shipbuilding center.

——— Florida's Most Famous Henries ———

During the late 1800s, at least two business leaders took advantage of the land given away by Florida's state government. Henry M. Flagler (1830–1913) and Henry B. Plant (1819–1899) built up Florida's coasts, boosting the state's economy and helping turn Florida into a major tourist attraction.

Flagler concentrated on Florida's east coast. One of his major accomplishments was to help organize the Florida East Coast Railway, which by 1912 stretched from Jacksonville all the way to Key West. Flagler also built hotels in Saint Augustine, Palm Beach, Miami, and other seaside cities.

Plant worked on Florida's west coast. He purchased a string of railroads that eventually connected Florida with the northern United States. In 1886 Plant bought a fleet of steamships to carry goods to and from Florida and the Caribbean islands. Plant also built hotels, including the lavish Tampa Bay Hotel.

At a Tampa cigar factory, workers select the best leaves to use as cigar wrappers.

Two deadly hurricanes, one in 1926 and another in 1928, put an end to Florida's boom. More than 2,000 people were killed in these hurricanes, which struck southern Florida by surprise.

The state saw more hard times with the beginning of the Great Depression in 1929. This slump in the nation's economy lasted about 10 years. Banks closed, railroad companies lost money, and tourism declined.

The nation's economy turned around during World War II (1939–1945). Florida became the site of more U.S. military bases. The state's usually clear skies allowed air force pilots to practice

During World War II, U.S. Navy pilots practiced flying bomber planes over Miami *(left)*. Astronauts on the *Apollo 11* spacecraft *(below)* were the first people to land on the moon.

takeoffs and landings almost daily. Florida's glitzy hotels were temporarily turned into hospitals and training camps.

After the United States and its allies won the war, many of Florida's military bases remained active. In 1950 the U.S. government established Cape Canaveral, a missile-testing site on Florida's Atlantic coast. In 1963 the National Aeronautics and Space Administration (NASA) opened the John F. Kennedy Space Center near Cape Canaveral. NASA's first goal was to put a person on the moon. The space center accomplished this mission in 1969.

The 1960s saw a great increase in Florida's population. As air conditioning became common, more people could tolerate Florida's hot summers, and elderly people from northern states moved to Florida to escape from the cold winters.

Thousands of other newcomers sailed from Cuba and Haiti, two island countries located south of Florida. These **immigrants** hoped to find better jobs, better homes, and more freedom than they had experienced in their homelands.

Air conditioning became popular in Florida's motels in the 1950s.

Hurricane Andrew reduced this trailer park in Homestead, Florida, to rubble.

In 1986 part of the space program at Cape Canaveral came to a halt. In January of that year, the space shuttle *Challenger* exploded just after take-off, killing all seven crew members. The accident marked the greatest tragedy in NASA's history.

Another disaster occurred in Florida in August of 1992. Hurricane Andrew struck the Atlantic and Gulf coasts with howling winds blowing 160 miles per hour. Andrew killed 40 people, destroyed billions of dollars worth of property, and left thousands of Floridians homeless and without food or water. Tent and trailer colonies were set up to provide homes, food, and clothing for those people who lost their property in the hurricane.

For more than a month during 2000, Florida was the center of national attention as Americans waited to find out who their new president would be. The contest between candidates George W. Bush and Al Gore was so close throughout the United States that Florida's results would determine the winner. But Florida's count showed that Bush led Gore by very few votes—so few that the state's crucial **electoral votes** could not be immediately awarded to either candidate. After five weeks of recounts and court challenges, the U.S. Supreme Court halted the counting. Bush was declared Florida's winner and became the nation's 43rd president.

PEOPLE & ECONOMY

Life in the Sunshine State

Chances are good that if you meet a Floridian on the street, you'll discover that he or she was not born in Florida. The Sunshine State attracts people from all over the world, and newcomers have made Florida one of the fastest growing states in the nation.

The state's population rose to nearly 16 million in 2000, having increased by 24 percent since 1990, when the population was about 13 million. Many Floridians live in one of the state's five largest cities— Jacksonville, Miami, Tampa, Saint Petersburg, and Hialeah. Tallahassee has been Florida's capital city since 1824.

Downtown Miami is a thriving economic center.

Although most Floridians were born in the United States, about one out of ten people in the state moved there from another country. Some Floridians were born in countries such as Great Britain, Germany, Canada, Cuba, and Puerto Rico. Puerto Rico became part of the United States in 1898.

A clarinet player from Bradenton, Florida, takes part in a marching band performance.

Newspapers and signs printed in Spanish are found throughout Miami. Many Cubans, whose native language is Spanish, settled in this city after making life-threatening journeys on small and over-crowded boats to escape difficulties in Cuba. Florida's **Latinos**, most of whom are of Cuban descent, make up almost 17 percent of the state's population.

African Americans make up 14 percent of Florida's population. Most Native Americans were removed to Oklahoma after the Second Seminole War, but small numbers of Seminoles remain in Florida.

Each year, millions of people visit the Walt Disney World Resort's Magic Kingdom in Orlando.

Mickey Mouse and his pals are such well-known residents of Florida that they might as well be included in the state's population figures. The world's most famous mouse came to Florida when Walt Disney World Resort opened near Orlando in 1971. Since then, Mickey Mouse, Minnie Mouse, Goofy, Donald Duck, and Pluto have entertained thousands of vacationers every year. But visiting the animated characters at Walt Disney World is only the beginning of what people can see and do in Florida.

Busch Gardens in Tampa is an adventure for all. A stroll through the zoo leads you past African lions and tigers. The amusement park in the gardens offers dozens of thrilling rides. At Parrot Jungle and Gardens in Miami, trained parrots and monkeys perform tricks. Near Orlando, Sea World of Florida is a splash when Shamu, the "Killer Whale," performs for audiences.

Visitors to Miami's Parrot Jungle and Gardens can see beautiful, rare animals such as these macaws.

A shuttle is prepared for launching at the John F. Kennedy Space Center.

John Pennekamp Coral Reef State Park off the island of Key Largo was the first underwater park established in the mainland United States. Those who aren't afraid of what might lurk in the sea can go diving to examine the reefs up close. Others can view the colorful formations from a glass-bottom boat.

In eastern Florida, along what is known as the Space Coast, people can imagine what it would be like to be an astronaut by visiting the John F. Kennedy Space Center. Just south of the Space Coast lies the Treasure Coast, where divers still find precious booty from Spanish ships that sank in the 1500s.

These are only a few of the hundreds of attractions in Florida. One of the state's most popular events is the Orange Bowl, a college football game played in Miami. The Gator Bowl in Jacksonville and the Florida Citrus Bowl in Orlando are other college football events held each year in the state.

(Professional sports teams in Florida include football's Miami Dolphins and Jacksonville Jaguars, soccer's Tampa Bay Mutiny and Miami Fusion, basketball's Miami Heat and Orlando Magic, and baseball's Florida Marlins and Tampa Bay Devil Rays.) Baseballs also fly through the air every spring, when 20 major league teams from cold, northern states come to Florida to warm up for the baseball season.

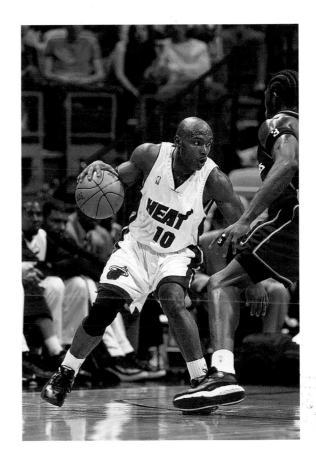

A basketball player from the Miami Heat heads for the basket.

When they aren't having fun in the sun, Floridians work in a variety of jobs. About 71 percent of Florida's workers have service jobs—that is, they help other people and businesses. Service workers in Florida include the lifeguards who watch over swimmers and the hotel desk clerks who give vacationers the keys to beachfront rooms. The agents

Restaurant employees are among Florida's many service workers.

who buy and sell resorts and retirement homes and the salesclerks who sell cans of sunshine to tourists are also service workers.

Some of Florida's workers have jobs with the government. They include the governor, national and state park workers, and employees at the John F. Kennedy Space Center. Florida is also a leading manufacturing state. Companies in the state produce equipment needed to run the space programs at Cape Canaveral. To make fertilizer, Florida continues to mine its large supply of phosphate rock. Many Floridians squeeze grapefruits, oranges, and lemons into juices. Oranges are also boiled to make marmalade.

Citrus farmers in south central Florida grow most of the nation's oranges—about two-thirds—along with tons of grapefruits, limes, tangerines, and lemons. Other fruits come from the state's banana trees and strawberry patches.

Florida produces more sugarcane and more houseplants than any other state. Tomatoes and cotton are other chief crops. Livestock farmers raise mostly beef and dairy cattle.

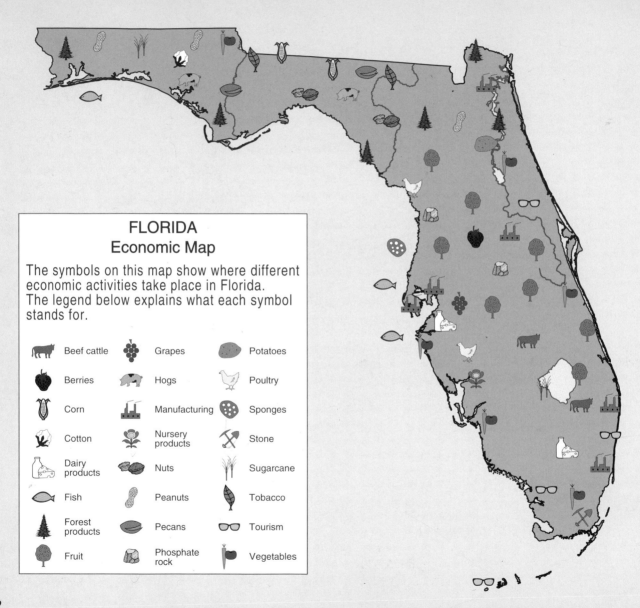

FLORIDA
Economic Map

The symbols on this map show where different economic activities take place in Florida. The legend below explains what each symbol stands for.

Beef cattle	Grapes	Potatoes
Berries	Hogs	Poultry
Corn	Manufacturing	Sponges
Cotton	Nursery products	Stone
Dairy products	Nuts	Sugarcane
Fish	Peanuts	Tobacco
Forest products	Pecans	Tourism
Fruit	Phosphate rock	Vegetables

The fishing industry in Florida makes millions of dollars catching fish and shellfish from the state's coastal waters. Shrimp, lobsters, and scallops bring in the most money. Popular saltwater fish include grouper, mackerel, and red snapper. Catfish is the leading fresh-water catch.

A large portion of Florida's fish, shellfish, citrus fruits, and other goods are shipped to other states. Tampa, along the Gulf coast, is the state's leading port, handling about 50 million tons of incoming and outgoing goods a year.

Raising beef cattle *(above)* is an important industry in parts of southern Florida. At an orange farm *(bottom right)*, oranges are gathered to be sent to the nation's produce markets.

53

Protecting Coral Reefs

Coral reefs thrive in Florida's warm, clear waters.

Florida is the only place in North America with a long line of coral reefs in its shallow coastal waters. Thousands of colorful reefs are located along the state's coast. In some places, the seawater is so clear and shallow that the beautiful patterns and colors of the reefs can be viewed from ashore.

Coral reefs flourish along Florida's coast because the waters are warm and clear. Every year, these reefs attract thousands of visitors who want to explore the delicate underwater coral gardens. But some of these people are careless and accidentally destroy some of Florida's reefs.

Coral reefs are made up of both living and nonliving elements. The foundation of a coral reef is

limestone. The limestone is actually produced by colonies of tiny sea animals called **coral polyps,** which secrete a coating of limestone around part of their bodies. When the colonies die, these limestone skeletons contribute to a reef's growth. Because polyps are so small, reefs grow slowly— only 1 to 16 feet every 1,000 years!

Because Florida's coral reefs are fragile, divers must be careful not to harm them.

Many types of plants and animals, such as these feather-duster worms, make their homes in Florida's coral reefs.

Coral reefs serve many purposes. They provide shelter, food, and breeding sites for many underwater plants and animals. They also break strong waves, naturally protecting Florida's coasts. As solid as they may seem, coral reefs are actually very fragile.

By simply standing on or scraping a coral colony, for instance, divers can start a chain reaction. Broken or scraped coral might become infected and die. The infection could spread and kill an entire colony. Boaters and fishers also start these infections by grounding their boats on coral reefs, hitting the reefs with anchors, or scraping them with fishing spears.

In addition, coral reefs, which need clear, clean water to grow, die quickly when exposed to pollution. Because water pollution comes from so many sources, including septic tanks and farms, it is one of the most difficult environmental problems to solve.

To help protect areas of coral, Florida opened the John Pennekamp Coral Reef State Park—the world's first underwater marine park—in the 1960s. In the 1970s, the U.S. government created what has become the Florida Keys National Marine Sanctuary—another area of protected reefs. Removing coral, anchoring or grounding boats on coral, throwing garbage into the water, using spear guns or wire fish traps, and even standing on coral are all against the law in the sanctuary.

Layers and layers of coral polyps make up this huge brain coral.

Despite the sanctuary's many restrictions, the government does make it possible for visitors to enjoy the reefs. People can still boat, swim, and dive in the sanctuary as long as they are careful. But the sanctuary may limit fishing, jet skiing, diving, treasure hunting, boating, and docking in areas most

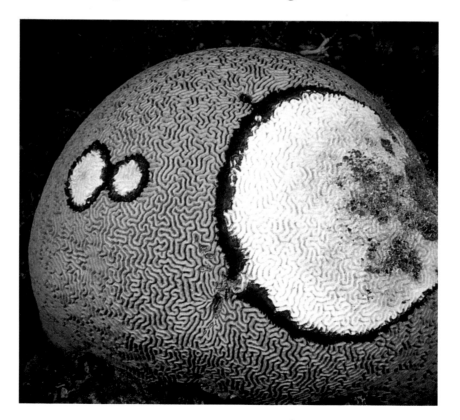

The white and brown patches on this brain coral are infected. The infection could kill all of the coral's living colonies if it continues to spread.

likely to be damaged from these activities. In the sanctuary, a warning not to stand on or around coral is distributed in English, Spanish, German, Japanese, French, and Italian. It's a simple message, reminding Floridians and tourists from around the world that in a matter of seconds they can destroy what took nature thousands of years to create.

The world under the surface of Florida's coasts is one of mystery and beauty.

ALL ABOUT FLORIDA

Key West is a popular vacation center.

Fun Facts

The southernmost city of the mainland United States is Key West, Florida. It lies only 90 miles north of the island nation of Cuba.

Florida is named in honor of Pascua Florida, an Easter festival held each year in Spain. Spanish explorer Juan Ponce de León gave Florida its name because he landed there the day of the celebration.

One of Florida's rivers has left its mark in music history. The Suwannee River was the subject of Stephen Foster's song "Old Folks at Home" (also known as "Swanee River"). The tune is Florida's state song.

Sanibel Island along the Gulf coast is called the Shelling Capital of the Western Hemisphere. The beaches of the island are sometimes layered knee-deep with billions of seashells.

Gatorade gets its name from the University of Florida Gators. The popular sports drink was invented at the University of Florida.

The Florida Strawberry Festival is held each year in Plant City, Florida. The appropriately named city lies in Hillsborough County, where about 2,600 fruit and vegetable farms are located. The festival was founded by the Plant City Lions Club in 1930.

STATE SONG

Florida's official state song is "Old Folks at Home," also known as "Swanee River." It was written by Stephen C. Foster in 1851 and adopted by the state legislature in 1935.

OLD FOLKS AT HOME

by Stephen C. Foster

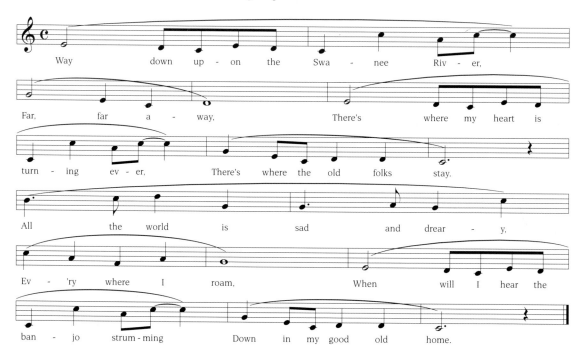

You can hear "Old Folks at Home" by visiting this website:
<http://www.50states.com/songs/florida.htm>

A FLORIDA RECIPE

Key Lime Pie gets its name from the
Florida Keys, a group of islands off the
southern tip of Florida. Introduced in
Florida in the late 1850s, this refreshing treat
is a dessert favorite in the state. On very hot days serve it frozen!

KEY LIME PIE

1 pre-prepared graham cracker crust (9 inches)
3 separated eggs
1 can sweetened condensed milk (14 ounces)
1/3 cup lime juice
1 teaspoon grated lime zest
1 cup whipped topping

1. Have an adult preheat the oven to 250° F.
2. Beat egg whites until stiff in a large bowl, set aside.
3. Beat egg yolks in a medium bowl. Stir in lime zest, condensed milk, and lime juice.
   Mix well.
4. Fold mixture into egg whites. Pour everything into crust.
5. Bake for 10 minutes.
6. Chill completely and add whipped topping, if desired.

HISTORICAL TIMELINE

10,000 B.C. Native Americans first arrive in Florida.

A.D. 1513 Juan Ponce de León searches for the Fountain of Youth in Florida.

1564 French Huguenot settlers build Fort Caroline.

1565 Pedro Menéndez de Avilés founds Saint Augustine.

1763 Spain gives Florida to Britain.

1783 Spain regains control of Florida.

1817 First Seminole War (1817–1818) begins.

1821 Spain gives Florida to the United States for $5 million.

1824 Tallahassee becomes Florida's capital.

1835 Second Seminole War (1835–1842) begins.

1845 Florida becomes the 27th state.

1861   Floridians supply foodstuffs to Confederate soldiers during the Civil War (1861–1865).

1868   Florida is readmitted to the Union.

1895   Henry Flagler establishes the Florida East Coast Railway.

1926   Florida's economic boom ends when a severe hurricane strikes the state.

1950   Cape Canaveral opens.

1963   The National Aeronautics and Space Administration (NASA) opens the John F. Kennedy Space Center near Cape Canaveral.

1969   *Apollo 11* is launched from Cape Canaveral.

1971   Walt Disney World opens near Orlando.

1986   Space shuttle *Challenger* explodes.

1992   Hurricane Andrew devastates southern Florida.

2000   In a historical but disputed election, a small majority of Floridians help elect George W. Bush to be U.S. president.

OUTSTANDING FLORIDIANS

Anthony Carter

Wallace ("Wally") Amos Jr. (born 1936) founded the Famous Amos Chocolate Chip Cookie Company in Los Angeles, California, in 1975. Wally's cookies became wildly popular after people learned that many Hollywood stars loved the taste. Amos was born in Tallahassee.

Anthony Carter (born 1960), from Miami, played football for the Minnesota Vikings and the Detroit Lions. Carter played in two Pro Bowls. While playing college football for the University of Michigan, he was named to the All-American team three years in a row. He retired from professional football in 1995.

Faye Dunaway

Faye Dunaway (born 1941), an actress from Bascom, Florida, first made it big as gangster Bonnie Parker in the 1967 film *Bonnie and Clyde*. She has played leading roles in many other movies, including *Chinatown*, *Three Days of the Condor*, and *Mommie Dearest*. Dunaway received an Academy Award for her performance in *Network*.

Gloria Estefan (born 1957), a Cuban American songwriter and singer, grew up in Miami. Estefan, who performs ballads and dance music with a Latin beat, has enjoyed popular success with songs in both English and Spanish.

Gloria Estefan

Chris Evert (born 1954) is a world-champion tennis player who grew up in Fort Lauderdale, Florida. The daughter of a tennis instructor, Evert began playing the game at age six. She won more titles (157) and matches (1,300) than any other player of her time. Evert retired from tournament competition in 1989.

Chris Evert

Dwight ("Dr. K") Gooden (born 1964), a pitcher from Tampa, joined the New York Mets in 1984 at the age of 19. In 1985 he became the youngest athlete ever to win the National League's Cy Young Award. His fastballs, traveling as fast as 96 miles per hour, have struck out many batters. Gooden retired from baseball in 2001.

Dwight Gooden

Ernest Hemingway (1899–1961) is remembered for his simple and honest writing style. Many of Hemingway's novels are based on his experiences in different locations, including the Florida Keys. While in Florida, Hemingway worked on *To Have and Have Not, A Farewell to Arms,* and *For Whom the Bell Tolls*—three of his most famous novels.

Ernest Hemingway

Zora Neale Hurston (1903–1960), a writer born in Eatonville, Florida, wrote *Mules and Men,* a collection of folktales about southern blacks living in rural communities. Her most famous novel is *Their Eyes Were Watching God.*

Zora Neale Hurston

James Weldon Johnson (1871–1938) wrote a well-known novel about racism called *The Autobiography of an Ex-Colored Man.* He also wrote the lyrics to the song "Lift Ev'ry Voice and Sing," which is considered a national anthem by many African Americans. In 1993 the song was published as an illustrated children's book. Johnson was born in Jacksonville.

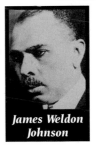

James Weldon Johnson

Charles Edward Merrill (1885–1956), from Green Cove Springs, Florida, began a small investment business in 1914. By 1941 it had grown to become Merrill, Lynch, Pierce, Fenner & Beane (later Merrill Lynch & Co.)—the largest brokerage firm in the world at the time.

Jim Morrison

Jim Morrison (1943–1971), a singer and songwriter, formed a rock band called the Doors in 1965 with organist Ray Manzarek. The group's best-selling albums include *Waiting for the Sun* and *L.A. Woman*. Morrison was born in Melbourne, Florida.

Osceola (1804?–1838) was a great American Indian leader. Born in Georgia, he was the leader of the Seminoles in Florida during the early part of the Second Seminole War (1835–1842). Osceola died in prison at Fort Moultrie, near Charleston, South Carolina.

John Pennekamp

John D. Pennekamp (1897–1978) helped establish Everglades National Park and John Pennekamp Coral Reef State Park. An editor of the *Miami Herald*, Pennekamp lived in Miami for more than 50 years.

Tom Petty (born 1952) is a singer, songwriter, and guitar player from Gainesville, Florida. In 1975 he formed the rock group Tom Petty and the Heartbreakers. Petty's best-known hits include "Refugee," "Free Fallin'," and "Mary Jane's Last Dance."

Sidney Poitier

Sidney Poitier (born 1927), from Miami, has starred in several films that address racial problems in the United States. His film credits include *The Blackboard Jungle* and *Guess Who's Coming to Dinner*. In 1963 Poitier won an Academy Award for his performance in *Lilies of the Field*.

Asa Philip Randolph

Asa Philip Randolph (1889–1979) worked as an activist to gain rights for laborers. Randolph persuaded Presidents Roosevelt and Truman to give African Americans a fair chance at government jobs. In 1957 Randolph became a vice president of a powerful labor union called the AFL-CIO. He was born in Crescent City, Florida.

Janet Reno (born 1938), from Miami, served as Florida's state attorney for 15 years, starting in 1978. In 1993 she became the first woman to be appointed U.S. attorney general, the nation's "top cop."

Janet Reno

Burt Reynolds (born 1936) spent much of his childhood in West Palm Beach, Florida. After a knee injury ruined his chances in professional football, Reynolds turned to acting. His performance in the 1972 motion picture *Deliverance* made him famous, launching him into starring roles in *Smokey and the Bandit* and a popular television show called *Evening Shade.*

Burt Reynolds

David Robinson (born 1965), from Key West, is one of the best basketball players of his time. Before being the first pick in the 1987 NBA draft, Robinson set more than 30 basketball records at the U.S. Naval Academy. In 1990 he was named NBA rookie of the year. He won the NBA championship with the San Antonio Spurs in 1999 and has been a member of three U.S. Olympic teams.

Mel Tillis (born 1932), a country singer and songwriter from Pahokee, Florida, has written more than 450 songs, including "Ruby Don't Take Your Love to Town."

Mel Tillis

Vicente Martinez Ybor (1818–1896), a native of Spain, built Tampa's first cigar factory in the 1880s, starting the city's cigar-making industry. Ybor City, a Cuban neighborhood in Tampa, was once a settlement for Martinez's factory workers.

Vicente Martinez Ybor

FACTS-AT-A-GLANCE

Nickname: Sunshine State

Song: "Old Folks at Home"

Motto: In God We Trust (unofficial)

Flower: orange blossom

Tree: sabal palm

Bird: mockingbird

Gem: moonstone

Animal: Florida panther

Saltwater fish: sailfish

Reptile: alligator

Date and ranking of statehood: March 3, 1845, the 27th state

Capital: Tallahassee

Area: 53,937 square miles

Rank in area, nationwide: 26th

Average January temperature: 59° F

Average July temperature: 81° F

Florida's state flag was adopted in 1899. The state seal sits in the middle, on a white background with a red cross. The red cross was added so that the flag, when seen from a distance, would not look like the white flag used by armies to signify surrender.

POPULATION GROWTH

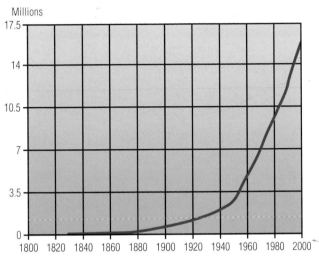

Millions

This chart shows how Florida's population has grown from 1830 to 2000.

Florida's state seal was adopted in 1868 and updated in 1985. It shows rays of sunshine and a sabal palm to represent Florida's warm climate; a steamboat to represent transportation; and a Seminole woman scattering flowers.

Population: 15,982,378 (2000 census)

Rank in population, nationwide: 4th

Major cities and populations: (2000 census) Jacksonville (735,617), Miami (362,470), Tampa (303,447), Saint Petersburg (248,232), Hialeah (226,419), Tallahassee (150,624)

U.S. senators: 2

U.S. representatives: 25

Electoral votes: 27

Natural resources: forests, limestone, petroleum, phosphate rock, sandy beaches

Agricultural products: bananas, beef cattle, cabbage, grapefruits, houseplants, lemons, lettuce, limes, milk, oranges, strawberries, sugarcane, sweet corn, tomatoes, watermelons

Fishing industry: catfish, clams, grouper, lobster, mackerel, oysters, scallops, shrimp, swordfish, tuna

Manufactured goods: aerospace and aircraft equipment, books, canned fruit, citrus fruit juices, communication equipment, computers, fertilizer, newspapers, X-ray equipment

WHERE FLORIDIANS WORK

Services—71 percent (services includes jobs in trade; community, social, and personal services; finance, insurance, and real estate; transportation, communication, and utilities)

Government—13 percent

Manufacturing—7 percent

Construction—6 percent

Agriculture—3 percent

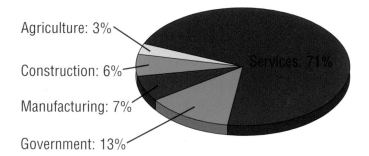

Agriculture: 3%

Construction: 6%

Manufacturing: 7%

Government: 13%

Services: 71%

GROSS STATE PRODUCT

Services—73 percent

Government—12 percent

Manufacturing—8 percent

Construction—5 percent

Agriculture—2 percent

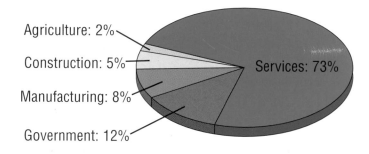

Agriculture: 2%

Construction: 5%

Manufacturing: 8%

Government: 12%

Services: 73%

FLORIDA WILDLIFE

Mammals: black bear, bobcat, deer, dolphin, Florida panther, gray fox, opossum, otter, rabbit, raccoon, skunk, squirrel, West Indian manatee

Birds: anhinga, egret, flamingo, heron, ibis, mockingbird, pelican, wood stork

Amphibians and reptiles: alligator, American crocodile, frogs, sea turtles, snakes

Fish: bass, bluefish, bream, catfish, clam, conch, crab, crappie, crayfish, grouper, mackerel, marlin, menhaden, mullet, oyster, pompano, red snapper, sailfish, scallop, sea trout, shark, shrimp, tarpon

Trees: ash, bald cypress, beech, hickory, magnolia, mangrove, maple, oak, palm, pine, sweet gum

Wild plants: azalea, bougainvillea, camellia, Carolina yellow jasmine, dogwood, flame vine, gardenia, hibiscus, iris, lilies, lupine, morning glory, oleander, orchids, poinsettia, red bud, sunflower

Alligators live in the wild swamplands of the Everglades in southern Florida.

PLACES TO VISIT

Castillo de San Marcos National Monument, Saint Augustine
Built more than 300 years ago by the Spanish, this fort is the site of the first permanent European settlement in the continental United States. It features museum exhibits, live cannon firings, and a Junior Rangers program.

Everglades National Park, southern Florida
Visitors can hike, camp, canoe, and spot alligators in this protected wilderness area.

Fort Caroline National Memorial, Jacksonville
French explorers attempted to establish a colony in 1564 at this site along the Saint Johns River. Their fort was destroyed by the Spanish, but it has been partly rebuilt for visitors.

Fort Matanzas National Monument, Saint Augustine
This fort was built in the 1700s by the Spanish so that guards could watch for enemies approaching from the south.

Gatorland, Orlando
More than 100 alligators can be viewed from this park's observation towers. If you're feeling brave, try the Gator Munch Meal at Pearl's Smokehouse.

John and Mable Ringling Museum of Art, Sarasota

Once the winter home of John Ringling, a partner in the Ringling Bros. and Barnum & Bailey Circus, this museum houses thousands of artworks of all kinds. It also contains artifacts related to circus history.

Kennedy Space Center Visitor Complex, Merritt Island

Learn how the United States space program launches satellites and shuttles, meet a real astronaut, or tour a model of a space station's living quarters. Visitors may even have a chance to watch a space shuttle launch.

Museum of Discovery and Science, Fort Lauderdale

Check out the world's largest captive Atlantic coral reef, and explore ecology, technology, and space through hands-on exhibits.

SeaWorld Adventure Park, Orlando

Visitors can get splashed by the park's most famous resident—Shamu—and see polar bears, feed dolphins, and ride a floorless roller coaster.

Walt Disney World Resort, Orlando

This famous resort features four theme parks, EPCOT Center, many thrill rides and exhibits, a movie studio complex, and, of course, Mickey and Minnie Mouse.

ANNUAL EVENTS

Zora Neale Hurston Festival of the Arts and Humanities, Eatonville—*January*

Florida Citrus Festival, Winter Haven—*January or February*

Daytona 500 auto race, Daytona Beach—*February*

Silver Spurs Rodeo, Kissimmee—*February*

Bike Week, Daytona Beach—*February–March*

Flying High Circus, Tallahassee—*April*

Florida Folk Festival, White Springs—*May*

Fiesta of Five Flags, Pensacola—*June*

Florida International Festival, Daytona Beach—*July*

Days in Spain, Saint Augustine—*September*

Florida Citrus Bowl, Orlando—*December or January*

Gator Bowl, Jacksonville—*December or January*

LEARN MORE ABOUT FLORIDA

BOOKS

General

Chang, Perry. *Florida.* New York: Benchmark Books, 1998. For older readers.

Fradin, Dennis B. *Florida.* Danbury, CT: Children's Press, 1994.

Wills, Charles A. *A Historical Album of Florida.* Brookfield, CT: Millbrook Press, 1994.

Special Interest

George, Jean Craighead. *The Everglades.* New York: HarperCollins Children's Books, 1995. Award-winning author Jean Craighead George describes how humans have affected the plants, animals, and ecosystem of the Florida Everglades.

Kavasch, E. Barrie. *The Seminoles.* Orlando, FL: Raintree Steck-Vaughn, 2000. Learn about the culture, history, and modern life of one of Florida's Native American nations.

Porter, A. P. *Jump at de Sun: The Story of Zora Neale Hurston.* Minneapolis, MN: Carolrhoda Books, Inc., 1992. This biography of the popular writer discusses her efforts to promote African American culture.

Sherrow, Victoria. *Hurricane Andrew: Nature's Rage.* Hillside, NJ: Enslow Publishers, Inc., 1998. This book describes Hurricane Andrew's devastation of the southeastern United States in 1992 and the recovery efforts that followed.

Walker, Sally. *Manatees.* Minneapolis, MN: Carolrhoda Books, Inc., 1999. Walker details the manatee's life cycle and behavior as well as the ways humans are trying to save it from extinction.

Fiction

Bernardo, Anilu. *Jumping Off to Freedom.* Houston, TX: Arte Publico Press, 1996. A boy and his father encounter adventure and hardships as they journey by raft from Cuba to Florida. For older readers.

Di Camillo, Kate. *Because of Winn-Dixie.* Cambridge, MA: Candlewick Press, 2000. A dog helps 10-year-old Opal learn about her family and herself after she moves to a new town in Florida. A 2001 Newbery Honor Book.

Rawlings, Marjorie Kinnan. *The Yearling.* New York: Scribner, 1985. This Pulitzer Prize–winning classic tells the story of a boy named Jody, his pet fawn, and their life in the back country of central Florida. First published in 1938.

WEBSITES

www.MyFlorida.com
<http://www.myflorida.com>
At the official website of the state of Florida, viewers can find information about Florida's government, state issues, and tourism.

Visit Florida
<http://www.flausa.com/>
Florida's official tourism site, available in several different languages, allows viewers to take a virtual tour of the state and provides information about travel destinations and events in Florida.

The Florida Times-Union
<http://jacksonville.com/>
Read about current events in the online version of this popular Florida newspaper.

Florida Kids
<http://dhr.dos.state.fl.us/kids>
Check out this website just for kids, featuring pages on history, state symbols, government, and even shipwrecks.

Florida Association of Museums
<http://www.flamuseums.org>
This website features links to online exhibits, gallery tours, and homepages for Florida's museums.

PRONUNCIATION GUIDE

Apalachee (ap-uh-LACH-ee)

Apalachicola (ap-uh-lach-uh-KOH-luh)

Calusa (kuh-LOO-suh)

Cape Canaveral (kayp kuh-NAV-ruhl)

Haiti (HAYT-ee)

Huguenot (HYOO-guh-naht)

Menéndez de Avilés, Pedro (may-NAYN-dayth day ah-vee-LAYS, PAY-droh)

Okeechobee (oh-kuh-CHOH-bee)

Okefenokee (oh-kuh-fuh-NOH-kee)

Seminole (SEHM-uh-nohl)

Tallahassee (tal-uh-HASS-ee)

Tequesta (tee-KWEHS-tuh)

Timucua (tihm-uh-KOO-uh)

Boating is a popular sport in Florida.

GLOSSARY

colony: a territory ruled by a country some distance away

coral polyp: a small, tube-shaped sea animal. The limestone skeletons of coral polyps form the hard base of coral reefs.

coral reef: a ridge of rocklike formations made up of billions of coral polyp skeletons

electoral vote: a vote cast in the electoral college. The electoral college is made up of a group of people called electors from each state. The electors choose the president and vice president of the United States. They are expected to vote for the candidate who has won the most votes in their state.

immigrant: a person who moves into a foreign country and settles there

Latino: a person living in the United States who either came from or has ancestors from Latin America. Latin America includes Mexico and most of Central and South America.

marsh: a spongy wetland soaked with water for long periods of time

peninsula: a stretch of land almost completely surrounded by water

plantation: a large estate on which crops are grown by workers who live on the estate. In the past, plantation owners usually used slave labor.

Reconstruction: the period from 1865 to 1877, during which the U.S. government brought the Southern states back into the Union after the Civil War. Before rejoining the Union, a Southern state had to pass a law allowing black men to vote. Places destroyed in the war were rebuilt and industries were developed.

INDEX

PHOTO ACKNOWLEDGMENTS

Cover (left): © William A. Blake/CORBIS; Cover (right): © W. Perry Conway/ CORBIS; PresentationMaps, pp. 1, 8, 9, 52; © Kevin Fleming/CORBIS, pp. 2–3; © Kit Kittle/CORBIS, p. 3; © Richard Jacobs/Root Resources, p. 4 (detail), 7 (detail), 18 (detail), 43 (detail), 54 (detail); Buddy Mays/TRAVEL STOCK, pp. 6, 44, 73; © Karlene V. Schwartz, p. 7; © Adam Jones, pp. 10, 16, 55, 57; Frederica Georgia, pp. 11, 17, 47; NE Stock Photos: © Clyde H. Smith, p. 12; James E. Sirvaitis, p. 13; Rick Poley, pp. 15, 60; Florida State Archives, pp. 19, 21, 22, 24, 28, 29, 32, 34, 35, 36, 38, 39 (left), 40, 67 (second from top), 67 (bottom), 68 (second from top); © Peter Randall, p. 23; Library of Congress, p. 25, 31; Independent Picture Service, pp. 27, 68 (bottom); Neg. No. 327045, Dept. of Library Services, American Museum of Natural History, p. 30; NASA, p. 39 (right); © Frank Siteman, p. 41; © Paul E. Clark, pp. 45, 54, 80; Jerry Hennen, p. 46; © Brian Carr, p. 48; © ALLSPORT USA/ Eliot Schechter, p. 49; © Bill Bachmann, p. 50; Olive Glasgow, p. 53 (top); © D. I. MacDonald, p. 53 (bottom); Alex Kerstitch, p. 56; © Franklin & Kathy Viola, pp. 58, 59; Tim Seeley, pp. 63, 71, 72; Rick A. Kolodziej, p. 66 (top); Hollywood Book & Poster Co., pp. 66 (second from top), 68 (top), 68 (second from bottom), 69 (second from top); Munawar Hosain/Fotos International/Archive Photos, p. 66 (second from bottom); © Carol Newsom, p. 66 (bottom); Houston Astros, p. 67 (top); Fisk Archives, Fisk University, p. 67 (second from bottom); Department of Justice, p. 69 (top); MCA Records, p. 69 (second from bottom); Special Collections, University of South Florida Library, p. 69 (bottom).